Organic
Weed Management

HANDS-ON ORGANICS

The Northeast Organic Farming Association (NOFA) is one of the oldest organic agriculture organizations in the country, dedicated to organic food production and a safer, healthier environment.

The Hands-on Organics series began with gift to NOFA/Mass and continues under the NOFA Interstate Council with support from NOFA/Mass and a generous grant from Sustainable Agriculture Research and Education (SARE). It is designed to present a comprehensive view of key farming practices from the organic perspective to benefit more advanced farmers and gardeners—and those looking to make the transition.

Organic agriculture has deep roots and represents a complex ecological and holistic paradigm that stands in bold contrast to the industrialized agriculture dominating today. It's critical that organic farming get a fair hearing in the public arena—and that farmers have access not only to the real dirt of organic methods and practices, but also to the concepts behind them.

Many farmers and gardeners have arrived at their own best methods to suit their situations of place and pocketbook. These manuals are designed to help practitioners review and reconsider their concepts and practices in the light of holistic biological realities, classic works, and recent research. Often, a few between-the-ears adjustments are what is needed to tackle intractable problems and bring one's operations into balance. The information presented can generally be scaled up or down to fit each grower's particular needs.

Organic
Weed Management

Steve Gilman

Foreword by Lynn Byczynski
Illustrated by Jocelyn Langer
Cover illustration by Robin Wimbiscus

CHELSEA GREEN PUBLISHING COMPANY
WHITE RIVER JUNCTION, VERMONT

Edited by Jonathan von Ranson. Assistance provided by these volunteer
NOFA farmers:

Julie Rawson
Lynda Simkins
Donna Berlo
Rich Williams
Beth Henson
Chris Holopainen

This book was first published in 2000 by NOFA/Mass., 411 Sheldon Rd.,
Barre, MA 01005
First Chelsea Green edition, November 2002.

Designed by Janet North.

Printed in Canada.
First printing, November 2002.
05 04 03 02   1 2 3 4 5

Chelsea Green Publishing Company
P.O. Box 428
White River Junction, VT 05001
(800) 639-4099
www.chelseagreen.com

Contents

FOREWORD. vii

by Lynn Byczynski

INTRODUCTION ix

To weed/a weed; Committing herbicide; Beneath the surface;
The oats test

CHAPTER ONE: WEEDING OUT WEEDY CONCEPTS 1

Weeds as enemy; Weeds as indicators; Weeds as guardians;
Weeds as beneficial medicinals; Lion's teeth

CHAPTER TWO: NATURAL FARMING 11

Hospitality for beneficials; Strip insectary intercropping; Biostrips;
Mow and blow

CHAPTER THREE: WEED CONTROL STRATEGIES 21

Stale seedbed; Stirrup hoe; Perennial problems; Timing your timing;
Anticipating weeds; Data overload; To mulch or not to mulch;
Hungry mulches; Living mulches; Opaque solar film

CHAPTER FOUR: WEEDEATING MACHINES 37

Biological effects of machines; A sense of humus; Conservation tillage;
Cultivators; Good resources

CHAPTER FIVE: CONCLUSIONS 47

REFERENCE NOTES 53

BIBLIOGRAPHY 54

INDEX 57

Foreword

Weeds are part of the equation when you farm or garden, and you have two choices about how to approach them. You can think of them as a pest problem, an obstacle to your success, a black cloud that is forever hanging over your garden. Or you can accept them as rightful members of the garden ecosystem, just one more type of plant that you need to observe and learn about in the endlessly delightful challenge of growing food and flowers.

I choose the second option, though I must admit that some days the first approach comes more naturally. Weeds are rarely welcome in my flower fields, but I have learned enough about them over the years to know when they are a genuine problem and when they're not worth worrying about.

For example, I know some people who obsess about henbit, a low-growing, purple-flowered plant that flourishes in the bare soil of late winter and early spring. I met one fellow who apologized about the henbit in the grassy area beside his driveway. He had tried everything, he told me—meaning every herbicide labeled for it—but with no success. I personally found the henbit charming, a stripe of purple in the brilliant green of spring's first growth. Furthermore, I knew that the henbit wasn't hurting anything except his misplaced pride. It's a cool-season weed that flourishes for a few weeks, then goes away. Even in a field of early flowers or vegetables, henbit merits only one cultivation, just enough to uncover the soil to let it warm and get the crops up and growing. After that, the crop plants predominate and the henbit eventually goes dormant from the heat.

But that knowledge didn't come from a book. It came from more than a decade of growing a particular set of crops on a particular piece of land. Like so much else in farming and gardening, learning about weeds depends as much on experience as on facts. My weeds won't be the same as your weeds, just as my crops and scheduling won't be the same as yours. As a result, what works for me might not work for you, and vice versa. Only by careful observation and trial can you learn what weed-control strategies will work best in your own situation.

This book, then, is not a how-to manual in the conventional sense of telling you how to control specific weeds. Instead, it's a guide to "how to think" about weeds, and it provides an overview of various non-chemical weed control options. Steve Gilman, an experienced farmer whose production talents are much admired in the market gardening world, has set forth a sensible philosophy about weed control. His gentle, holistic approach will help you put weeds in perspective. And once you've got the right outlook on these "plants growing in the wrong place," you will be much better equipped to know when and how to remove them, outwit them, or live with them.

Lynn Byczynski

Lynn Byczynski is the publisher and editor of the monthly newsletter Growing for Market. *She is the author of the bestselling book,* The Flower Farmer *(Chelsea Green, 1997), and grows flowers commercially at Wild Onion Farm in Lawrence, Kansas.*

Introduction

Weeds can be one of the most daunting adversaries organic farmers and gardeners ever have to deal with. After all, building a lush, fertile soil high in organic matter can benefit all sorts of plant life besides your crops. Weeds happen. Wild plants have evolved to not merely survive but proliferate. A single redroot pigweed can produce over 20,000 seeds that may remain viable in the soil seedbank for 20 years or more awaiting a shot at germination. Weeds will always be with us—indeed they play a highly important role on the planet, including soil protection; offering room and board for beneficial insects, soil animals, and microbes; and promoting a healthy, biodiverse landscape.

From a holistic perspective, weeds may not be the main problem at all, but a symptom of unbalanced soil or adverse growing conditions. The key to dealing with weeds is learning how to manage and work *with* their considerable energies in the context of whole systems. At its most basic, it requires rethinking the whole nature of weeds and our attitudes and approaches toward them.

To weed/a weed

Dictionary definitions show how deeply rooted the negative perceptions of weeds have become in our consciousness. Appreciating their true nature, so you can effectively utilize their attributes and keep them under control, can require some major between-the-ears adjustments. Weeds have had bad press for a long, long time, some of it well-deserved. Most basically, weeds are plants in the wrong place. They may even be the offspring of crops you sowed yourself—volunteer tomatoes coming up in the onions, buckwheat in the spinach. More often, they're the wild ones that have established a toehold or more and won't let go: annual pigweeds, smartweed, and lambsquarters; persistent perennial quackgrass and thistle; and nasty exotics like arrowleaf tear thumb.

Weeds and the negative attitudes surrounding them have worked their way into our language and need some weeding out of their own. Definitions of the verb "to weed" include clear out, uproot, cut down, remove, and "to eradicate as harmful or useless."[1] The act of weeding is often presented in terms of unending combat. Any "weed" (noun) growing in the vicinity is depicted as useless, unwanted, invasive, and without economic value. However, most of these same weeds viewed in the context of beneficial wild plants have a long and illustrious history as health-giving "herbs" with considerable medicinal and nutritional qualities, many uses, and high economic value. For instance, the weed St. John's wort (*Hypericum* spp.) has poisonous effects on cattle, but the same plant has a long-established medicinal usage for moderating depression and has become an intensely cultivated, high-value herbal product.

Committing herbicide

It's important to keep in mind the incredible value of wild plants in ecological systems. Bare soil is a losing proposition—open to erosion by wind and rain, desiccation by the sun, the oxidation/depletion of humus, and rampant biocide of microorganisms. The 2-foot-deep topsoil of the once-pristine prairie soils in the Midwest now averages under 4 inches; the rest has been permanently lost to the winds or sent down muddy waters into the sea just in the short time this country has been in business—all in the name of an industrial "efficiency" misapplied to agriculture.

The industrial mindset is clear: the only good weed is a dead weed. Chemical herbicides are viewed as a crowning achievement of modern agriculture. Crops are now being genetically engineered to be compatible with existing herbicides—Roundup Ready® soybeans join biotech cultivars of herbicide-tolerant corn varieties planted to millions of acres around the world. The efficacy of herbicides at first glance neglects to factor in the considerable economic and environmental "side-effects," however.

Beneath the surface

While it's immensely seductive to think all your weed problems can be solved with a spray, a look into the root zone shows a much different story. A presentation on the proper usage of herbicides compared slides of corn roots. The overdosed rootlets were "burned" and almost devoid of the tiny root hairs responsible for gathering soil nutrients, but what was even more instructive was that the corn root slides showing the proper use of herbicides showed a minimal number of root hairs too. The control rootlets, taken from corn growing in fertile soil without herbicides, were lushly covered with rootlets along their entire length.

In addition to putting stress on the crop's basic ability to nourish itself, herbicides have extensive biocidal effects on hosts of other life-forms beyond the targeted weeds. Impacts on plant life, bees, birds, insects, animals, and humans, as well as on microflora and fauna such as earthworms, beneficial bacteria, and fungi (including mycorrhizae) can completely alter the biological landscape. Pesticides also generate a phenomenon known as *secondary pest production*—all the pests that were previously held in check by diverse beneficials are freed to proliferate once their natural enemies are wiped out by the pesticides. The herbicide chemicals routinely decimate soil microorganisms and, in conjunction with synthetic fertilizers, actually destroy soil fertility.

The oats test

The use of herbicides severely limits the ability to rotate to a different crop family, leading to such deleterious practices as growing continuous corn, year after year. Try to introduce a broadleaf vegetable crop and it will be doomed to failure. Farmers or gardeners contemplating working fields with a recent history of herbicide use should first try the oats test. Fill 4-inch pots with topsoil samples from the areas in question, sow regular oats, keep moist, and observe what happens. Oats are very susceptible to herbicide damage—if nothing germinates within a week, or if the growth appears stunted or burned, then it will be necessary to cleanse the soil with a series of compatible cover crops. On herbicide-treated corn land, for example, a grass-based cover crop (corn is a grass) such as Sudax (a sorghum/sudan grass hybrid) can remediate the soil and provide copious quantities of organic matter to build tilth and fertility. The three-year no-chemical transition period required by organic certification programs reflects such realities for soil replenishment.

Finally, with millions of acres worldwide currently under agrochemical management, this means that most of our productive farmland—and our food supply—is 100 percent dependent on petrochemical inputs. Literally, no chemicals = no crop. With worldwide oil production due to peak and then turn downward in the next decade, this has definitive implications for long-term food security and sustainability worldwide. Clearly, major changes are needed, now.

One
Weeding out Weedy Concepts

When exploring the wide range of materials available on weed control it's important to keep an eye open to where the proponents are coming from and an ear tuned to money being made or axes grinding. How weeds are depicted to begin with can then justify how they should be dealt with. The underlying assumptions, however, may not necessarily be true.

In fact, there is a broad spectrum of attitudes about weeds—from archenemy to valuable ally. Even within the overall sustainable-organic mindset there are many positions in between.

Weeds as enemy

Weeds have generally been considered the "enemy" because they can easily compete with crops for nutrients, moisture, and sunlight—and they can win. Throw in the age-old competitive philosophy—us versus them—and you have the basis for today's conventional agriculture. Add in an industry-engendered estrangement from and mistrust of nature and the battle is joined. Warfare is the ultimate competition, a fight to the death against a purposely vilified enemy until the battles are won and the true "winner" emerges. Battling Nature (literally ourselves and our environment) is the ultimate lose-lose scenario, however—essentially self-destructive, and particularly schizophrenic.

Meanwhile, there are lots of careers at stake and money to be made on the supply side, not only for the input manufacturers but also for legions of researchers, dealers, and extension agents. The recent consolidation of agribusiness corporations gives them increased clout to call the tune, both economically and politically.

Conventional farmers have been referred to as "money launderers" for the agrocorporations because the majority of their income and most of their governmental crop support payments are directly turned over to agribusiness to pay for the ag inputs needed to produce the crop. What farming income remains is subject to the vagaries of the weather and skewed markets brought down by overproduction and indentured contract arrangements.

Furthermore, when nature itself is viewed as the enemy or, in our hubris, something to be improved upon, the results become highly skewed. We humans are of nature too. While the competitive school holds that whatever we humans do is ultimately correct because we are (obviously) nature's supreme expression of being, we've seen all too well how easily we can pollute our own nest and adversely affect the planet, ergo ourselves. Cartoonist Walt Kelley's character Pogo had it right: "We have met the enemy and he is us." Organic, ecological agriculture embraces the alternative paradigm, the cooperative one. We are of nature, and better get better at it.

Weeds as indicators

The fact is, weeds possess ample positive attributes. Certain indicator weed species can by their very presence tell you a lot about specific soil conditions. The pigweeds and lambsquarters indicate a cultivated, rich soil, for instance, so at least you know you're doing a good job with fertility management! On the other hand, horsetail (*Equisetum arvense*) likes soggy soil—time to pay attention to drainage.

A primary source for weed indicator information is the booklet, *Weeds and What They Tell*, by Ehrenfried Pfeiffer, published by the Bio-Dynamic Association. In it, Pfeiffer details the underlying soil conditions many weeds prefer—including droughty, poorly drained, acid, highly acid, poorly cultivated, salty, hardpan, presence of potassium, absence of lime, and so on. Also presented are a number of "dynamic" plants. That same horsetail, for instance, has a high silica content with antifungal properties useful for controlling damp-off and other diseases in the greenhouse.

Weed	*Soil Properties*
bindweed	hardpan
buttercup	inhibits clovers
chicory	deep, good soil
clovers	low in nitrogen
coltsfoot	heavy, wet, acidic
cornflower (blue)	high lime content
cornflower (pink)	acidic
docks	wet, poorly drained
daisy	heavy, acidic
dandelion	heavy, acidic
goldenrods	sandy, dry
lambsquarters	cultivated, dry

Weed	*Soil Properties*
mullein	acidic, low fertility
mustards	hardpan
horsetail	poor drainage, acidic
meadowsweet	wet, poorly drained
mosses	wet, poorly drained
nettle	fertile, acidic
pigweed	cultivated, fertile
plantains	heavy, wet, acidic
purslane	cultivated, fertile
quackgrass	hardpan
ragweed	indicates nothing
spurge	dry, sandy
thistle, Canada	heavy
wild carrot	sandy, low fertility
wild strawberries	acidic
yarrow	low in potassium

(Source: *Weeds and What They Tell*)

Weeds are *weeds* only from our human egotistical point of view, Pfeiffer says,

> . . . because they grow where we do not want them. In Nature, however, they play an important and interesting role. They resist conditions which cultivated plants cannot resist, such as drought, acidity of soil, lack of humus, mineral deficiencies, as well as a one-sidedness of minerals, etc. They are witnesses of man's failure to master the soil, and they grow abundantly wherever man has 'missed the train'—they only indicate our errors and Nature's corrections. Weeds want to tell a story,—they are Nature's means of teaching

man, and their story is interesting. If we would only listen to it we could apprehend a great deal of the finer forces through which Nature helps and heals and balances and, sometimes, also has fun with us.[2]

Despite touting their value, Dr. Pfeiffer comes down firmly on the side of weed combat and eradication in cultivated areas and even ventures into using chemical controls against virulent weed species. Overall, however, he demonstrates the immense value and knowledge to be gained from nature's wild plants while outlining hands-on practices for controlling them with cover crops and cultivation.

Weeds as guardians

Around the same time Sir Albert Howard (known as the Father of Organic Agriculture) was working with composts in Indore, India (1910), Joseph Cocannouer was carrying out soils research at the University of the Philippines. Based on his further soil conservation work worldwide, his book, *Weeds: Guardians of the Soil* (1950) has become an organic classic. Weeds, in Professor Cocannouer's viewpoint, serve immensely important and critical functions in the environment.

- Their deep-searching roots pump up trace elements and minerals from the depths of the subsoil, making them available to subsequent crops.
- They break up hardpan in the lower soil horizons, allowing following crops to feed more deeply.
- They "fiberize" the soil and provide beneficial friable soil tilth conditions for soil microorganisms.
- Weeds are excellent indicators of underlying soil conditions and deficiencies.

- Weeds' deep-diving roots and soil capillary action help shallow-rooted crops survive drought.
- As companion crops they assist weaker-rooted crop plants to get to otherwise unavailable nutrients.
- Weeds gather nutrients and minerals, keeping them from being lost to erosion and making them available for subsequent crops.
- They are tasty wild foods—delicious and highly nutritious.

Cocannouer's approach to weeds is part of his "Togetherness Principle"—developed long before the concept of ecology became established in our thinking.

Though we may not be conscious of it, or even wish to admit it, our success very largely depends on the understanding we have of Nature's law of togetherness, and our adherence to it. Every phase of agriculture is dependent upon the workings of this law. It is well enough to talk about the mechanization of crop production, but unless the machine is made to work in harmony with the togetherness law there will be trouble. The agricultural machine can be made to work with Nature instead of against her. . . . An ideal soil world, with all the factors functioning healthily and efficiently, is the togetherness law in superb manifestation. In such a soil there is supreme harmony: the necessary mineral elements are there, and the necessary gases. There is the indispensable fiber to regulate structure and to provide food and warmth for the live factors. These factors, along with a host of others all working together, furnish and prepare the ingredients that are to be sent up to the food factory of the leaf, where they will receive the final processing. Again, let anything interfere with the soil-world laboratory—interfere with the togetherness law down there—and discord becomes evident . . . : the soil itself is thrown out of balance; the leaf factory may be forced to turn out an unbalanced food product. Animal life, which is at the mercy of the plant world, finds itself responding with weakened body structures. The animal world gets sick—and all because something interfered with the togetherness law in the soil world.[3]

Weeds as beneficial medicinals

Despite the competitive cast to the European/Western tradition, the deep lore of herbalism and medicinal botanicals is beginning to make a resurgence among health-conscious consumers. Many virulent agricultural weeds are among the most powerful remedies. Rank weeds such as stinging nettle, burdock, dandelion, lambsquarters, purslane, chickweed, and even poison ivy possess valuable medicinal qualities.

While the magic-bullet elixir approach of allopathy continues to predominate in this country, in some other cultures herbal medicine has achieved great sophistidation. Weleda herbal products in Germany, for instance, certifies both the organic/biodynamic farms that grow the herbs as well as the physicians who diagnose and prescribe them. Traditional Chinese medicine practitioners have extensive schooling in the preparation and use of herbal remedies, many of which have been used for millennia.

Lambsquarters

It should not be surprising that weeds possess such powerful attributes. Through eons of natural selection and adaptation to harsh and highly competitive environments, they have successfully evolved to be strong and hardy. Many are deep-rooted and able to withstand long periods of drought and other adverse conditions. In contrast, most crop varieties are bred to be coddled and cultivated and couldn't survive long in the wild if left to their own devices.

Just the same, a medicinal botanical growing in the wrong place can be just another weed to be rid of. Their fierce natural competitiveness and adaptability to hostile conditions (including your own eradication efforts) makes them powerful adversaries. It is important to know and respect their qualities. On a basic level, using them as food or medicine can connect you to their deeper qualities and turn the hostile foreigners into more friendly, useful allies.

Lion's teeth

A flush of dandelions in the spring, as just one example, might well be tolerated on ground being readied for later-season, warm-weather crops. The bright yellow blossoms are the first major pollen/nectar food source of the season for wild pollinators and provide an insectary habitat to help breed populations of beneficial insects to later serve the crops. Researchers have observed 93 different insects feasting on their bounty. The deep-rooted dandelions can also punch drainage holes down through hardpan and help alleviate compaction while pumping subsoil nutrients and minerals back up into the top "A" soil horizon for use by subsequent crops.

The roots, leaves, and flowers of the dandelion (from the French *dent de lion*, or lion's tooth) have been regularly used as food and medicine for over a thousand years. The first greens of the season cooked as a potherb or steeped as a tea are a powerful spring tonic, just the thing to energize and acclimate stiff, winter-weary farmers trying to get back into the swing of the new season. The root crowns and rosettes of very young leaves can be prepared in salads or steamed as highly nutritious vegetables. Once we're privy to their secrets, dandelions and their brethren will never be considered mere weeds again, although they still need to be managed in the crop zones through tillage and cultivation.

Two
Natural Farming

Significantly broadening the spectrum of weed management approaches is *The One-Straw Revolution*, a book by Masanobu Fukuoka, published in 1978. A farmer for most of his long life, Mr. Fukuoka began his career as a laboratory-based microbiologist and specialist in plant diseases. A series of revelations based on his observations of the vigor of plants growing in the wild caused him to challenge the conventional specialized scientific views and return to his ancestral lands to work out his holistic conceptions. As word of his work spread, he demonstrated his techniques—and impressive results—to a steady stream of visitors and researchers, as well as to students and apprentices who came to work and experience his natural farming approach firsthand. The book was translated into English by a number of those students, and Wendell Berry contributed a preface for the Rodale Press edition.

While Mr. Fukuoka's methods are totally specific to growing successions of rice crops, vegetables, fruit, and winter grains in his locale (on the Japanese island of Shikoku), his concepts significantly broaden the paradigm of agricultural cooperation with nature. His overall approach and vision is valuable and immediately applicable to farmers and gardeners around the world.

In the fall, he intersows seeds of rice, white clover, and winter grains such as rye onto mowed but unplowed (for 25 years) ground and then covers the area with a thick layer of rice straw. While the rye (or barley) sprouts immediately, the rice stays dormant until spring. Meanwhile, the citrus harvest—including mandarin oranges—takes place on the adjoining mountainsides from November until April.

The mature grain is harvested in May, its straw immediately spread on the field to build soil fertility and preserve humus. While the traditional rice growers hold water in their fields all summer long, Mr. Fukuoka retains it only during the June monsoons to weaken the weeds and sprout the rice. When the fields are drained, the clover soon recovers and provides a dense living mulch to protect the rice and crowd out remaining weeds. The accumulated soil organic matter holds ample moisture so that no irrigation is necessary, and it also promotes vigorous rice crops, which easily get the best of any weeds that make it through. While the traditional and conventional growers face a full-time job all summer keeping their plots cultivated, fertilized, pest-free, and irrigated, Mr. Fukuoka just lets his fields go. The rice harvest is in October, and his yields are consistently as good as or better than those of other farmers using chemical or traditional methods.

Mr. Fukuoka has achieved what he calls "a balanced rice field ecosystem" that supplies its own fertility and pest control: one where stable relationships are built and maintained between the soil, the plants, and insects. His "Four Principles of Natural Farming" may be reduced to No Cultivation, No Fertilizer, No Weeding, and No Chemicals. He had long since observed that reducing cultivation reduced weeds and that the weeds themselves were valuable soil fertility sources in conjunction with other green manures and straw. Fertilizers, however, could overstimulate and weaken the crop. He further demonstrated that the augmented, biologically diverse habitat harbored beneficial insects and soil organisms—making additional pest controls unnecessary.

Mixtures of vegetables and herbs were also grown on the orchard slopes among the trees. The established clover and weed understory is mowed and covered with straw—crop seeds are then sown in holes poked into the soil. Corn and soybeans are interplanted together. Some seed is soaked in a mixture of fine clay and water: the dried coating protects it from mice and birds when broadcast (then mulched), to germinate and take hold with no tillage. Some vegetable varieties were allowed to go wild and untended, yielding harvests and sowing themselves year after year. Again, the balanced cropping ecosystem consistently provided pest and disease control.

Natural farming methods must necessarily tune in to one's own climate and growing conditions, but the underlying paradigm of learning to work with nature is universally valid and applicable. While Mr. Fukuoka's warm and humid climate with predictable rainfall (the monsoon season) is highly conducive to such an approach, it was only after years of intense observation and experimentation that he brought his agricultural system into harmony with his surroundings. The fact is, his area is no less weedy than other climate zones and may be even more so than temperate climates. Yet weeds are no longer a problem for him, indeed, they contribute greatly to soil fertility and a balanced ecological habitat.

Hospitality for beneficials

While the growing conditions here in the northern reaches of North America are vastly different from those in southern Japan, some growers are developing natural farming techniques appropriate to this climate. The essence remains the same—utilizing the natural benefits of weeds as mulches, as fertility and organic matter sources, and as rich habitat for beneficial insects and microorganisms.

The organic approach already provides some long-term beneficial ecological effects. In contrast to the experience of conventional farms, where insect, weed, and disease pressures build up over time because of increasing pest resistance to chemical pesticides and herbicides, mature organic farms and gardens exhibit the opposite effect. As the whole farm ecosystem comes into balance, more and greater numbers of beneficial species become part of the landscape. Systematically utilizing the habitat potential of wild plants to provide increased "room and board" for beneficials—the insects, earthworms, mycorrhizae, disease-suppressing microbes, etc.—is a valuable holistic, permanent approach to agriculture. Over time, such farms are becoming balanced ecological entities where disease and pests are naturally controlled by indigenous populations of beneficials, sometimes without the need for additional inputs.

The Permaculture movement, initially concerned with creating a more sustainable "permanent agriculture" based on such concepts back in the 1960s, has generally evolved into a comprehensive landscaping approach for households, integrating dwellings with plants and landscape to create a site-specific energy-efficient, ecological design. Many basic Permaculture concepts hold true for agriculture, however, and there is a rich, well-established body of knowledge to draw from.

Strip insectary intercropping

While organic growers have long recognized the value of maintaining diverse habitat near their fields and gardens, a method called *strip insectary intercropping* brings such habitat right into the field alongside the crops on a permanent basis. Many of these insectary plants are indigenous weeds that are allowed to flourish within a controlled management system.

To begin with, the entire growing area is laid out in permanent raised beds, generally 48 to 52 inches wide for ease of workability, with 24- to 30-inch pathways in between. Raised beds effectively provide a compaction-free zone which is quick to warm up in the spring. The loose, friable, highly organic soil tilth promotes both drainage and moisture-holding capacity and enhances root growth.

On my farm, the beds are formed and later maintained by a 52-inch Kuhn rotovator rear-mounted between the wheels on a 38-horsepower tractor set up to straddle the beds. Heavier-duty tractor-powered spading machines are also excellent bed formers/maintainers and may be better suited to more fragile soil types than my clay loam. Additional cultivation of the beds is done with an Allis Chalmers "G," also set to wide wheel spacing.

Some time ago I began questioning the time and energy needed to keep the strips between the beds clean-cultivated, let alone the ramifications of creating erosion zones. What has evolved over time are permanent sod strips, sown partially to Dutch white clover, but also containing a hugely diverse number of perennial grasses, wild herbs, and wildflowers that grew in naturally. Nasty perennial weed species such as quack grass and thistle were mostly eliminated by repeated cultivations before the beds were formed, however.

Biostrips

These "biostrips" serve a multitude of holistic functions beyond just controlling weeds. They bring a diverse, protective habitat and food supply for beneficial insects and microorganisms right into the field alongside the crops. A highly diverse mix of grasses, legumes, naturalized herbs, and wildflowers, the strips yield four to five major cuttings per season. A mow-and-blow method distributes the clippings onto adjoining beds, where they can be tilled in as feed for soil microbes or left on the surface as a moisture-preserving, weed-excluding mulch.

The beds provide solid, muck-free footing for the tractor and keep the farmer out of the mud when the fields are wet in the spring or after heavy rains. Any potential compaction from equipment (or feet) is confined to the biostrips, where it is supported by the extensive sod root systems. There's a positive visual aspect as well. Visitors (or Community Supported Agriculture shareholders) coming to the farm are often anxious about

A biostrip growing between young corn and sunflowers.

where to walk and are relieved when asked to please walk on the grass. Kids understand the concept immediately, and even pets can be trained to stay on the strips—and out of the crops.

The system places over one-third of the field acreage in permanent, year-round, "no-till" cover, fully preventing erosion and preserving soil organic matter. By definition these strips no longer contain "weeds," even though many of the grass, wildflower, and wild herb species are often categorized as weed species in other contexts. Here their function is cooperative, not competitive.

The planting beds themselves are routinely sown to quickly growing cover crops ("catch crops") like buckwheat or annual ryegrass whenever there's an opening—after spring crops such as spinach or kohlrabi are done, for example, or over the course of the summer where annual soil-building cover crops (such as cowpeas, berseem clover, or fava beans) are part of the crop rotation schedule. Winter cover crops like oats, hairy vetch, and winter wheat or rye give full protection to the beds for the rest of the year. The combination of the biostrips, dense crop canopies, and various cover-cropping strategies means all the soil is well protected for most of the year.

The land area given over to the biostrips is more than offset by the increased growing capacity of the beds themselves. The beds are able to accommodate much more intensive crop spacings, resulting in considerably higher plant densities and yields per acre for most vegetable crops. The resulting denser plant canopies then shade and protect the bare soil in the beds, conserving moisture during droughty periods. Such intensive plantings can also significantly increase yields on a per acre basis for those with a limited land base. Totally free from compaction, the beds can become high-fertility zones (fed by the mown clippings from the biostrips) with ample nutrient- and moisture-holding capability. Looseleaf lettuce, for example, is traditionally grown in single rows 12 to 18 inches apart with the plants spaced at 10 to 12 inches apart in the rows. Properly conditioned 52 inch beds can easily accommodate 6 rows (6 inches apart) with the lettuce planted 6 inches on center.

Larger plants, such as brassicas, do well in a triangulated three-row system conducive to hoeing or other mechanical cultivation. Additionally, when the plants mature, a leaf canopy forms over the beds to reduce weed pressure and minimize evaporative water loss. Row spacing can be intensified to 15 inches apart, with plants spaced 15 to 18 inches apart in the row.

Crops that require or benefit from hilling (such as potatoes, leeks, and sweet corn) can be planted on 30-inch centers. All these spacings are easily accommodated by standard cultivating equipment, although modifications have to be made to fit the bed system.

A hand "gridder," consisting of a 4 x 6-foot piece of plywood with handles attached and properly spaced bolts projecting through to leave a soil imprint is a handy tool to get the spacings right. Two people lift and swing the gridder along from either side of the bed, stepping on it to leave impressions in the soil as they go. Tractor-drawn mechanical models consist of rolling drums with brackets or bolts welded on in the correct configuration.

When the biostrips aren't mowed, the "wildflowers of the week/month" that grow in become important pollen and nectar food sources for beneficial insects and wild pollinators. The strips are bright yellow with dandelions in the spring, white with Queen Anne's lace in late summer, and blue with asters in the fall—with a host of others in between. Each wave of wildflowers is mowed before going to seed, except for the white clover, which is let go to help increase the stands.

The biostrips also offer protective habitat—right in the field, side-by-side with the crops—for the beneficials. For pest species it's literally a hostile jungle out there, with enemies lurking everywhere. The permanent strips also provide an overwintering habitat for large populations of beneficials. It is important to allow regrowth and wildflower development. A frequently mowed "lawn" between the beds provides a minimal or negative habitat.

All the beds are best numbered and spreadsheets used to manage rotations so that no bed is planted back to the same crop family for at least three years. Also, crop families are kept spaced at least several beds apart to maximize plant community diversity and prevent monocropping situations that can breed up pest populations.

The sod strips maintain a deep-rooted connection to the falling water table in the heat of the summer, providing a positive upward hydraulic action that also benefits the more shallow-rooted crops in the beds between. Mycorrhizae, a beneficial soil fungus association that prevails in highly organic soils and sod communities, are able to reach in and colonize the beds from the adjoining biostrips, forming symbiotic relationships with the roots of the crop. In exchange for carbohydrates supplied by the plant, their interconnected networks act as pipelines, bringing ground water and nutrients (especially phosphorus) up to the crop plants. Mycorrhizae also have the ability to extract additional mineral nutrients from the stones and rocks in the soil, thus saving the need to purchase additional mineral supplements and amendments.

Mow and blow

A "mow-and-blow" system utilizes a heavy-duty rotary mower to periodically cut the biostrips and blow the biomass material directly onto the adjoining beds as a mulch, or as a food source for soil microorganisms when rotovated under. For tender crops such as lettuce, the mulch is blown onto the prepared beds first and the lettuce plugs transplanted through it. The lettuce matures before the strips need cutting again. Many crops, from squash to tomatoes, benefit from several mow-and-blow mulchings before fruit set. The biostrips become less vigorous/more dormant later in the heat of midsummer and do not need mowing—letting the habitat mature for the beneficials.

Attention is paid to potential incompatibilities. Queen Anne's lace may be a vector bringing the disease aster yellows to lettuce, for example. It is mowed down before flowering anywhere near the lettuce beds.

Once in balance, this system creates a deep reservoir of plant protection. It can transform the image of nature from a hostile force out to destroy and devour a farmer's crops into a powerful and awesome ally. Conventional intervention thresholds—where scouted crop damage or pest counts say it's time to spray—no longer hold true or even become necessary. The farmer, too, becomes an integral part of the whole system, privy to working with nature in a positive, creative, and inspiring way.

Three
Weed Control Strategies

All said and done, ally or enemy, weeds are still plants in the wrong place for our purposes and, given a shot at the upper hand, they can severely impact your present crops and sow problems for years to come. Some of the more virulent species definitely require a zero-tolerance approach.

Galinsoga, for instance, has no redeeming qualities whatsoever and should be removed whenever and wherever it is encountered. While passersby might only see a profusion of pretty low plants with tiny daisy-like blossoms that somewhat resemble a scentless chamomile, they cannot fathom the large greedy rootballs spreading out beneath the soil that make it such a voracious competitor. The afflicted grower, however, has experienced all too well how the newly cultivated weed seedlings can spontaneously reroot anywhere stem contacts soil or from a root trace inadvertently left in place, even in full, hot sun. The few stealthy plants that get to flower soon sow a dense mat of weeds that may require taking the area out of production for a season or two of cultivation and cover-cropping to rectify the problem.

While equally voracious, purslane at least has the attribute of being tasty and nutritious—and an increasingly marketable vegetable and salad herb in its own right. However, it has a marked ability to colonize areas through persistent rerooting and copious seed production from its nondescript flowers that stay hidden beneath the succulent, creeping foliage.

A good strategy for dealing with such powerful weeds is to map out the flare-up areas and then organize specific search-and-destroy missions that are not connected with any other tasks which might divert attention. Uprooting and spreading out weeds in the sun on rocks, or on some other surface where they cannot reroot, can finish the job and cement the commitment to eradication. Biodynamic growers take things one step further. Burning some of the weed material and spreading the ashes is said to inhibit the proliferation of the plant on a more basic plant energy level.

Finally, the best strategy of all is to deal with weeds while they are vulnerable seedlings. Poor Richard's admonition, "a stitch in time saves nine," is as applicable to weed control as it is to rent garments.

Growers would do well to adopt a special "time-lapse vision" and mentally fast-forward those innocuous, slender, wispy lambsquarters weed sprouts spied in the sweet corn, for example, into the dense growth of coarse, three-foot-high, raspy stalks laden with weed seed they will soon enough become. All is easier said than done, however. If the season is skewed by persistently wet weather in June, for example, cultivation becomes less effective and the weeds can get a big jump over the crops.

It is well to note that in adverse conditions chemical herbicides suffer in effectiveness as well. Calibrated for average, one-size-fits-all application, their efficacy can be quickly diminished by drought, too much rain, or temperatures that are too hot or too cold.

Stale seedbed

While the soil's weed seedbank may harbor an almost endless supply of long-lived wild plant seeds awaiting their shot at germination as nature intended, many of them lie too deep to sprout. The combination of light, heat, nutrients, and moisture all have to be present within specific parameters. The concept of the "stale seedbed technique" is to lightly cultivate the soil's surface to stimulate the weed seeds that are there to germinate and then cultivate again to kill them off before planting the main crop.

The secret is to confine the tillage operations to the soil's top inch; any deeper and you bring a new supply of weed seeds up into the germination zone. This method is particularly effective for fine-seeded crops such as carrots and herbs, where early competition from weeds can quickly set them back.

Stirrup hoe

One of the major weed control innovations of the past 50 years has got to be the concept behind the stirrup hoe. It is also known to gardeners and small-scale farmers as a "hula hoe" or "action hoe" because the double-edged thin steel blade is set to rock back and forth with a scuffling push/pull motion that cuts off tender weed seedlings just beneath the surface of the soil. Shallow-set tractor sweeps and mounted stirrups serve the same function on a larger scale.

The stirrup hoe successfully confines cultivation operations to the surface inch of soil without turning up or mixing in weed seed from lower layers. It is possible to literally exhaust the supply of weed seeds in the germination zone after two or three light cultivations—in effect creating a stale seedbed zone around the crop plants.

This is a vast improvement on the ancient hoe design which was built heavy to chop and bury young weeds—unfortunately, in doing so, it

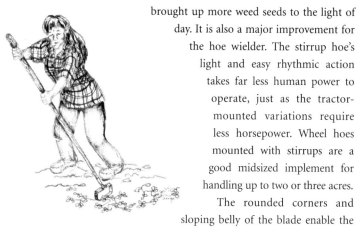

Stirrup hoe

brought up more weed seeds to the light of day. It is also a major improvement for the hoe wielder. The stirrup hoe's light and easy rhythmic action takes far less human power to operate, just as the tractor-mounted variations require less horsepower. Wheel hoes mounted with stirrups are a good midsized implement for handling up to two or three acres. The rounded corners and sloping belly of the blade enable the operator to get in close to tender crop plants without injuring stems or shallow roots. Even relatively unskilled farm workers can quickly get the hang of it. For growers using raised beds, certain layouts facilitate the advantages of the hoe. Large canopy crops like broccoli can be planted three rows to a bed. When the plants in the two outside rows are planted directly across from each other and the plants in the third, middle row are spaced in between, not only is there ample root room for each plant but a cultivating diagonal is formed. That is, a person armed with a stirrup hoe on each side of the bed can make short work of cultivating mature crops by each taking a diagonal line. The resulting crisscross pattern cleans out weeds on all sides of the plant.

Perennial problems

A further variation on the stale seedbed concept is called for in dealing with persistent *perennial weeds* such as quackgrass and various thistles, as well as beastly biennials like burdock. These plants tend to be much better established with extensive root systems and survival skills to match. The best way to propagate and spread a plot of quackgrass or Canada thistle is to till it up. In the process, the invasive white rhizomes reaching through the surface soil are chopped into pieces, and each small division then has the potential to sprout into a whole new plant, ultimately thickening the stand.

The secret to their resprouting ability lies in the nutrient storage capacity of the rhizomes themselves. The way to eradicate these weed problems is to repeatedly force the plants to draw upon their rhizome reserves, through persistent cultivation or a definitive mulch barrier followed by a series of cover crops, until they are exhausted. Better them than you: any field, bed, or garden area not brought under control initially will return to haunt you over and over again.

Bull thistle, burdock, and other biennial weeds are going to go to seed and die in their second year anyway. It is critical not to let them get beyond the flowering stage, or their copious seeding capacity will sow problems for years to come. These weeds can be controlled by persistent mowing to exhaust their root reserves. Repeated tillage can also be effective—if you have machinery sturdy enough to handle the job. Most mulches can't handle the task, however, for the weed growth is just too powerful.

Timing your timing

While your farm or garden may generally fall well between the broad lines delineating a particular zone on USDA's Plant Hardiness Map (my Zone 5 is last frost Memorial Day, first frost mid-September), your own microclimate is bound to have predictable aspects of its own, even with the widely skewed weather extremes we've been registering over the past decade or so. As indigenous species, weeds respond naturally to the coming of spring and can serve as valuable indicators to help determine the advancement of the season and planting times. Each growing season comes in with a life of its own—early, late, wet, dry, hot, cool, etc.—and going by the calendar date for a sowing and transplanting guide is not all that accurate. The organic method doesn't use soluble chemical fertilizers, therefore it depends on soil temperatures reaching above 60°F (16°C) to kick in the microbial activity that provides nutrients to crops. Keeping track of specific, local bioindicators, such as the appearance of the first dandelion blossoms, can tell you a lot about the delay or advancement of each particular season and the underlying soil conditions conducive for planting.

Keeping a daily farm or garden log is a hugely important research and planning tool in this respect. Recording the date of emergence or blossoming of wild plants in the spring—from the first swelling pussy willows, to coltsfoot blossoming, then bloodroot flowering in the woods, and on to the first major flush of dandelions in the fields—all paint a biological portrait of the relative earliness or lateness of each season. Depending on numerous site and environmental factors like elevation, northern exposure, prevailing winds, and southerly slope, these indicator plants only emerge when accumulated temperature conditions are appropriate in their specific area. Sometimes there are vast differences between one field and another on the same farm. Over time, your personal logs will provide invaluable information for working on your own place within the parameters and vagaries of each season.

Anticipating weeds

Because weeds are wild plants whose growth is sensitive to increasing temperature and light levels, their emergence as a problem in field or garden is also predictable. There's usually a grace period in spring, for example, before it's warm enough for the more voracious tender annual weeds to germinate. Timing your cool-weather crop sowings (onions, carrots, beets, kohlrabi, lettuce, etc.) early enough can give them a big head start before the weedy competition weighs in.

It's wise to schedule work time to address the first major flushes of weeds when you know they will be coming in, come heat or high water—and set aside time in your summer cropping workload to deal with them. Around here (Zone 5) the pigweeds and lambsquarters start to take off in mid-June and, unless addressed immediately, become a major problem.

Of course, skewed weather conditions such as heavy spring rains and flooding can delay early crop plantings. Then when things finally dry out everything happens at once anyway. So much for schedules. Here again, your daily log is a valuable planning tool: the more you can map out an overview of predictable occurrences the better you can deal with them.

Data overload

Biologically based agricultural systems involve a myriad of complex relationships between soil, plants, environment, and humans. In comparison, conventional chemical management is a gross oversimplification and highly reductionist, even as it embraces the high-tech trappings of so-called Precision Agriculture. You don't necessarily need overhead-satellite GPS computers on board the tractor to pinpoint your weedy zones, for instance, although the conventional mindset is that nature can ultimately be controlled if you can just muster enough technology against it.

Appropriate biological data and data management is even more critical for organic farms and gardens. Besides the daily log, another good tool to construct is a basic farm or garden map with transparent overlays that visually depict yearly rotations, soil amendment additions, and areas with pressure from specific weeds, diseases, and pests. It can save a lot of rummaging through back pages and also prevent needless field work. It's probably not a good idea to sow carrots in last year's corn patch where the lambsquarters got out of hand, for example. The weed pressure will just be too competitive for such a fine-seeded crop. A glance at the weed overlay sheet would suggest it would be much better to cultivate the area a few times, put in a thick summer cover crop such as buckwheat to smother the weeds and build up the soil—and prepare the area for next year's carrots.

Simple computer spreadsheets—nothing more than grids of columns and rows—are also a valuable way to record, file, and visually retrieve growing information that can be regularly updated and printed out for field use. While ornate systems can be developed to contain and present valuable information—and there are some pricey software packages available to help do the job—the bottom line for busy growers is ease of data entry and retrieval, or else it can become just another burdensome task that gets neglected 'midst the demands of a busy growing season.

To mulch or not to mulch

In terms of weed control, mulches are successful only insofar as they can cover and protect bare soil and prevent weed seeds from getting the light they need to germinate. Additional properties such as reduced tillage requirements, moisture retention, and soil temperature moderation, along with providing habitat for beneficials and building soil organic matter, can make mulching a very valuable practice.

One main barrier is having a ready supply of relatively clean mulch material available ahead of time—and the means to deliver and spread it. Larger farms with appropriate forage harvesting equipment for livestock, for instance, can cut and chop fresh alfalfa or haylage, blow it into a self-unloading wagon in one area of the farm and then haul and deposit it alongside nearby vegetable crops without much handling, although a certain amount of hand labor may be needed to rake it in around the plants. While a nearby municipal leaf dump may provide an almost inexhaustible source of excellent mulch (and compost) material, the loading, hauling, unloading, and spreading requirements may severely limit its usefulness.

Although bales of spoiled hay may hold the allure of being an inexpensively available and easily transportable local resource for small-scale farmers and gardeners, they are generally laden with weed seed, and in the name of weed suppression you may instead end up sowing major weed headaches for years to come. Commercial straw is cleaner but more expensive for applications of any scale, and you might also end up sowing a grain crop among your vegetables, as there's usually some seed still present.

Sometimes mulch materials show up in unlikely places. My farm is located near a lake laden with a Eurasian milfoil weed problem. The rampant growth is kept in check all summer with paddle wheel harvester boats that cut the weeds off underwater. Conveyors then load the weeds onto the boat and later off-load them onto dump trucks back on shore. Years ago, I could get tons and tons of material delivered free for compost and mulch. Now my farm is on a waiting list as other area farmers, landscapers, and gardeners have discovered its value, not the least of which is that any aquatic weed seeds that might be present in the milfoil can't germinate on dry ground.

Like gold, mulch is where you find it—and from the soil's point of view it is just as valuable a commodity for preventing erosion and building organic matter and fertility as it is for preventing weeds. Farms usually are located in areas with ample selections of inexpensive organic waste materials for mulch and compost. Those farms with split livestock/crop operations may be able to produce everything they need right on the farm.

Hungry mulches

Another consideration with organic mulches is that they are materials already embarked on a long-term process of decomposition. The highly carbonaceous materials that make for a good, durable mulch (leaves, straw, sawdust, woodchips even) contain woody cellulose and lignins—plant structures that require considerable amounts of nitrogen to break them down. Unless you add in an extra nitrogen-rich soil amendment before laying down the mulch, the carbonaceous materials may gobble up surface soil nitrogen reserves for their own purposes, at the expense of germinating and seedling crops. This same effect can also be seen after applying unfinished compost, for example—the crop plants slow down their growth and begin to yellow, a sure sign of nitrogen deficiency.

In northern zones there is a timing factor to take into account as over-wintered or early-applied mulches can keep the soil too cold, suppressing the biological activity that drives the whole organic system. Many key soil organisms remain inactive or dormant below soil temperatures of 60°F (16°C). For example, strains of a native beneficial fungus, *Trichoderma*, which colonize crop roots (providing disease control and enhancing root growth), grow too slowly below 60°F (16°C) to provide effective biocontrol. Bacteria vital for the efficient mineralization (release) of nitrogen optimize in the 70° to 100°F (21° to 38°C) range, although they start to become active in soil temperatures as low as 40°F (4°C).

In the North, mulch opening (zone tillage) or removal strategies become necessary to help directly warm the soil. Overwintered crops like garlic also profit by pulling aside heavier mulches to enhance biological activity in the root zone. Replacing it again later in the spring helps provide the critical weed control needed by all alliums and helps maintain constant moisture conditions for optimal growth.

A special soil thermometer with a 6-inch probe is an indispensable tool for growers looking to get an early spring start. While some cold weather crops such as early peas or onions can compensate, others such as lettuce, early brassicas, and carrots profit by the addition of soil amendments containing more soluble, readily available nutrients. Foliar and soil applications of fish emulsion and seaweed extracts are particularly useful in cold soils.

During the heat of the summer, mulches can help keep the soil cooler and more moist and can prolong the productivity of the crop. Mulched midseason broccoli, for instance, will often yield copious harvests of side shoots for long periods compared with their unmulched brethren that soon bolt to seed.

Living mulches

A living mulch is one that you intersow into the crop. It's a lot easier broadcasting cover crop seed into the vegetable rows or beds after the last cultivation than bringing in and laying down quantities of bulky mulch materials. Large farms sometimes sow rye from aircraft into their vast corn acreage. When the corn is harvested the rye has already filled in the understory, protecting the soil, sequestering excess leachable nutrients, and preventing erosion.

Smaller-scale growers can easily do the same with an over-the-shoulder, hand-cranked broadcast seeder or a tractor-mounted rig. Sometimes casting cover crop seed by hand is the best way to intersow into maturing crop canopies and, in this mechanized age, is an experience not to be missed. Grasping handfuls of seed, repetitively swooping your arm, rhythmically releasing and letting them fly (continually correcting for nuances of stride and windage) while moving through the field are motions farmers have practiced for millennia.

Living mulches require ample soil fertility to begin with or they can outcompete the crops for scarce nutrients and moisture—and this is their main drawback. They are excellent for capturing and holding any excess nitrogen, though, which is only destined to leach out of the root zone into the groundwater and streams.

Their competition with the crops for moisture and nutrients is relative, however. Repeated mechanical cultivation exposes the soil to erosion and literally burns up (oxidizes) soil organic matter. It also creates a vacuum where weeds are primarily positioned to take advantage of the fine seedbed prepared in the process. And when the crops grow too big to cultivate any further, the ensuing weeds may be even more voracious and competitive than living mulches.

Modern agriculture has come down solidly on the side of eradicating competition to crop growth (while ignoring the myriad "side effects" it creates above and below ground). This scorched-earth thinking overshadows the many beneficial cooperative and synergistic effects diverse plant and soil communities can bring to each other. Spongy soil tilth with ample organic matter and deep-diving cover crop root systems hold more moisture for the benefit of crop and living mulch alike, while protecting the soil against drying winds and baking sun.

Sowing living mulch sowed into aggressive crops like pumpkins and winter squash, in addition to corn, is a time-honored practice. Cover crops are broadcast around the crops and between the rows at the final cultivation, just before the plants send out runners (at which point you won't be able to get back to work the soil again).

Annual ryegrass—not the tall, overwintering grain rye—is an inexpensive, fast-germinating turf seed that quickly produces a grassy cover to fill the bare-soil vacuum and keep out weeds. In northern climates it will generally winterkill before going to seed and won't become a future weed problem in itself. It can be controlled by mowing if it survives a mild winter, however.

The aforementioned **grain rye** is much more competitive but is a favorite choice sowed in aggressive crops like corn and pumpkins because it is *allelopathic*—it exudes specific compounds from its root system that chemically suppress weed seed germination. Rye undersown into corn in later summer tolerates the shady conditions under the crop canopy and continues to grow well after the corn is harvested, right up until the ground freezes. It breaks dormancy in early spring and is usually plowed down or tilled in when it is 8 to 12 inches tall. It will eventually grow 3 to 4 feet tall before heading up to seed. For this reason, growers on wet, low-lying, or clay soils that preclude early tillage may decide to grow oats (which winterkill) instead. Facing a too-tall, overmature rye crop in a wet year can take the field out of crop production for weeks, as the mowed and tilled woody stems need yet more time to decompose before a crop can be planted.

Dutch white clover is one of the best living mulches, although the seed is considerably more expensive than that of other living mulch plants. It has the bonus legume effect of being able to fix nitrogen in its root nodules to build soil fertility. You should also purchase the specific rhizobia inoculant to coat the seeds before sowing. These bacteria are the work horses that colonize the root zone to capture nitrogen from the atmosphere.

Plantain, lambsquarters

Dutch white is very effective under corn or late-season brassicas—cabbage and Brussels sprouts especially. Its low-growing habit doesn't interfere with the crop, while its density keeps out weeds. Since it is a long-lived perennial and because of the expense factor, it may be wise to keep it on as a cover crop in your rotation through the following season and maximize its soil-building effects. It is able to spread itself by its creeping stolons (stems), while its numerous white blossoms are a prodigious pollen source for bees and beneficial insects. Mowing before the blossoms set seed will prevent it from becoming a weed problem itself, though it is not hard to get rid of by cultivation.

In general, other clovers such as mammoth red, berseem, crimson, and alsike are better suited as full-fledged cover crops rather than as living mulches because of their bigger size and competitiveness. Current research is looking to the turf industry, where noncompetitive grasses and fescues are being bred to produce quick cover (as nurse crops to protect slower-germinating quality turf grasses) and then to go dormant after their initial growth.

A further promising practice under experiment by several garlic growers is planting the clovers into a living mulch of oats. Seed oats (regular feed oats allow certain percentages of weed seed in the bag) sown by mid-September grow to 6 inches tall or so by the end of October when it's time to plant the garlic. Rows of narrow slits are cut into the soil through the living oats with cultivator or planter shanks, and the garlic is planted into the slots and closed over. The oats soon resume their growth and may get to 10 inches tall before winterkill, depending on how mild the season is. The garlic lies protected by the dense matted thatch of dead oats throughout the winter—which also serves as an effective weed barrier/mulch come spring and into summer. By then, the garlic is fairly easily harvested through the decomposed material.

Opaque solar film

Cold soil adversely affects the warm-climate crops that would prefer to grow a few hundred miles south. Coupled with a relatively short North Country growing season, tender varieties of melons, squash, cucumbers, and eggplant might have to be bypassed completely without the use of "opaque solar film," a.k.a. good old black plastic, and its newly developed infrared-transmitting offspring. These wavelength-selective mulches allow near-infrared light to pass through to warm the soil while screening out the visible light spectrum needed by weeds to grow, providing the crop with lush, more tropical growing conditions.

This solar mulch is also effective at holding in soil moisture—as long as the soil is wet before the plastic is laid down. Otherwise the material will shed much needed rainfall and the crop will suffer. Here, drip irrigation installed beneath the plastic becomes a necessity.

The more permanent woven-polypropylene weed-barrier landscaping fabrics are needle-punched to let moisture through and are suitable for perennial plantings. Some growers use precut lengths for early and late crops in hoop houses, for instance, and they pre-punch the material to accommodate the proper plant spacing for the particular crop. After harvest, the lengths are rolled up, labeled and stored until the next season comes around for that crop. Taken care of and removed from sunlight when not in use, the fabric can last five years or more.

Sooner or later the story with all agricultural plastics is that there's a disposal problem as well as all the petroleum pumping, refining, and processing that goes into making it to begin with. Specialized recycling centers that accept clean expanses of greenhouse poly for reformulation, for instance, aren't interested in soiled ground-applied films. Photodegradable plastics, including cornstarch-formulated films, while touted as the ideal disposal solution by agribusiness manufacturers, only break down so far in the field; that's why they are prohibited by organic certification programs. At the end of the season sunlight causes them to flake apart and finally break down into small particles, but the powdery remains persist in the soil along with heavy metal catalysts used in the manufacturing process, including nickel and iron.

A further caution about using plastic mulches: the habitat they create may radically favor pests over beneficials. Research on eggplant[4], for example, shows that the vast expanses of shiny plastic beneath the plants is the equivalent of a biological desert. Not only are the crop plants highlighted and made more visibly attractive to pests, but also the lack of a protective understory and habitat offers no cover for beneficials. Replicated comparisons showed a much higher count of Colorado potato beetles on the plastic-mulched eggplant than on the same varieties grown in bare soil. Eggplant mulched with straw or sown to living mulches of annual ryegrass or Dutch white clover after two cultivations (after the soil was allowed to warm up) showed the least pest pressure of all.

Four
Weedeating Machines

There's no doubt that mechanical advances have delineated the history of agriculture—from the planting sticks used in ancient times to today's satellite-guided precision planters. These developments have led us to the wholesale industrialization of agriculture. Farmer (and thus consumer) dependency on highly mechanized equipment as well as huge quantities of chemical and genetic inputs have become the dominant paradigm. Essentially, however, the reductionist industrial approach is more or less constantly at odds with the ecological realities of holistic biological systems—to the long-term detriment of our food quality, health, and environment.

Many of the farming methods we take for granted today evolved to fit the demands and limitations of the machinery, not necessarily to meet the intrinsic biological needs of the crops themselves. The practice of planting crops in rows, for example, was developed initially to give space for the horses or oxen to step, with the cultivators fanned out behind them. While today's monster tractors can pack hundreds of horsepower into one machine, they still require tire space to get through the fields without injuring the crops. However, the compaction alone from such weighty machines can severely damage soil structure and will harm crop growth over time. Sooner or later, an even bigger tractor will be needed to work the compacted soils to accomplish the same work, and so on.

Once started, the industrial approach takes on a life (and a self-justifying necessity) of its own. It makes good sense, under this approach, to remove all the hedgerows to gain larger workable acreage without having to turn the machines around as much, just as it's "smart" to plant in vast monocrops so you don't have to keep changing implements in order to work it. From the biological point of view, however, destroying the hedgerow habitat severely impacts populations of beneficials, and monocropping (with the use of pesticides, which select for chemically resistant pest species) is a great way to rapidly breed up major pest problems. Now repeated applications of more and more toxic insecticides are necessary to save the crop. And so on, each fix requiring another one further down the line. When the concomitant health and environmental side effects are factored in, this paradigm can hardly be considered efficient.

Biologically based approaches, on the other hand, keep the whole ecological system in mind. Consider the elegant synergy of the "Three Sisters" agriculture used by Native Americans hundreds of years ago, where corn, squash, and beans were interplanted to the same field. The beans were sown around the corn stalks and used them as trellises to climb on for support. In the soil, the heavy-feeding corn benefited from the nitrogen-fixing action of the beans. The squash, sown between the hills of corn and beans, crowded out weeds, provided a moisture-conserving canopy, and protected the soil. The corn's copious pollen production served as a food source for legions of beneficial insects and pollinators, providing definitive pest control. Overall, the richly biodiverse habitat made it difficult for any one pest species to gain a toehold to begin with. From a holistic viewpoint,

Three Sisters agriculture is both efficacious and environmentally beneficent.

From a production standpoint, however, intersown crops are difficult to work with tractors and the like. Similar positive biological effects can be achieved by growing mixes of crops and habitat plants next to each other in the field, while allowing for various degrees of mechanization. It doesn't take too many hours of slaving away by hand under the hot sun to consider quicker, less labor-intensive approaches to the necessary tasks. The real problem might be knowing when to stop. Many a farmer has succumbed to "hardware disease"—an addictive need for more and more highly mechanized (and expensive) implements to accomplish the same job. Beware this mindset because it can progress to the point where the farm's financial and biological bottom lines are negatively impacted and the demands of the equipment begin to rule.

Biological effects of machines

When choosing mechanized systems it's paramount to consider the biological effects of that mechanization, and to be aware of the alternatives to conventional machines, which abound. Regular cultivation, for instance, can rapidly oxidize away organic matter and deplete humus. Strip-till options may be the way to go. (Options in mechanical tillage systems are explained in the "Conservation tillage" section in this chapter.) Soil structure may be systematically destroyed by overreliance on a rotovator, especially on lighter, sandy-loam soils. Perhaps a rotary spader is the better investment. Stirrups and sweeps can replace conventional cultivators—they not only require less horsepower to operate, but leave deeper-down weed seeds alone, away from the surface germination zone. Using chisel plows overcomes the problems of the old moldboard plow (which buries organic matter and weed seed alike) and addresses the problems posed by E. H. Faulkner back in the early 1940s in his classic book, *Plowman's Folly*.

A word about maintenance—it takes time, constant attention, and money. Murphy's Law (if things can go wrong they will) has a particular agricultural corollary: farm equipment always breaks down when you need it most. The bottom line is that beginning farmers should realize that some types of machinery create more problems than they solve, while experienced farmers might profit by taking a more holistic view of their practices and reassessing their operations from a biological standpoint.

A sense of humus

Not the least of the ongoing problems created in the name of weed control are the negative effects of tillage. Each pass with a cultivator aerates and mixes the soil and literally burns up (oxidizes) soil organic matter. Decomposition bacteria are greatly stimulated. Over time, the practice can severely deplete humus.

As a gauge, most soil testing labs will give you the organic matter content of your soils as a percentage of total soil content. Five percent is an excellent proportion in temperate soils, but this level is difficult to maintain while farming, even with regular applications of compost, green manure, and cover crops. Soils containing less than 2 percent organic matter may not be able to support the critical biological functions of a fertile soil system at all. The soil's organic matter content, therefore, is the bottom line to verify the biological effectiveness of your agricultural practices. Unfortunately there are no easy tests for humus.

Humus itself is difficult to define and quantify. Its chemical and structural composition varies considerably from soil to soil, and it often can appear very different. Visually, it is hard to distinguish from other forms of organic matter. Like petroleum deposits, native humus is a finite vestige of ancient organic residues laid down eons ago, decomposed and microbially processed into a dark, biologically stabilized organic essence. It has a huge capacity to hold nutrients and moisture and is the ultimate tilth habitat for supporting immense populations of soil life—the microorganisms and soil animals that constitute soil fertility. Its structural properties also help glue soil particles together and guard against erosion.

The process of *humification*—the building up of stabilized indigestible residues produced by microbes feeding on soil organic matter and mineralizing nutrients for their own metabolisms—is quickly dislodged by many of the mechanisms of agriculture. Farmland humus is not easily built up or replaced, even under best management practices. Often the most we can do is protect and maintain it and not diminish it further. Indeed, much of the famed productivity of the Midwest farmlands has been at the direct expense and permanent loss of the soil's store of organic matter and humus. Industrialized agriculture has been living high on the hog, squandering the natural wealth of some of the richest soils in the world for a relatively short-term gain. (Remember that Europeans and their descendents have only been in this land for a few hundred years.)

Today, relatively cheap agricultural petroleum products act as humus substitutes, but all signs point toward severe dislocations in their availability and price in the coming decade. By then, on most of our farmland the natural constituents of soil fertility will be close to exhaustion. A negative (but true) view of the History of Agriculture is one of civilizations periodically depleting their soils and then moving on. The problem now is there's nowhere left to go.

Conservation tillage

The good news for conventional agriculture, thanks in a large part to conservation tillage practices, is that the U.S. soil erosion rate has been reduced by around 38 percent since 1982. The bad news is that since 1995 the reduction has leveled off. Almost 2 billion tons of soil is still being lost annually and fully 30 percent of the nation's farmland was reported to be eroding excessively.[5] Much of this soil loss occurs in the name of weed control—herbicides leave bare soil in their wake.

Conservation- or reduced-tillage practices attempt to staunch erosion by maintaining large amounts of crop or cover crop residues in the field to protect the soil. Technological advances in machinery for large-scale operations are offering alternatives to herbicides that are definitely a step in the right biological direction. Moderate-residue, high-residue, and maximum-residue cultivators make use of heavy-duty sweeps that undercut weeds and leave residues on the surface. While the largest units may weigh in at two tons or more, the small-scale units (requiring much less horsepower to operate) utilize spring-cushioned C-shanks or S-tines that vibrate to aerate the soil and dislodge weeds.

With **No Till** weed management, low-growing cover crops are herbicide-killed and crops are sown into the stubble with heavy-duty planters. This method effectively controls erosion, especially on hilly ground, and also keeps weeds at bay. It remains highly dependent on herbicides, however, keeping things agribusiness-as-usual while cloaking injurious biological practices in the good name of conservation tillage.

Furthermore, farms north of Pennsylvania or so experience problems with crop seed germination and early spring growth using this method, however, because the complete cover can keep the soil too cool and wet through the spring. Even when herbicides are not used and the cover crops are killed by special cutters (that scalp the cover crop from its roots and leave it in place as a mulch) or are flail-chopped or flame-killed, cold soils still present a problem. Much of the successful research for these methods is being done in Maryland and Georgia, where the warmer conditions make it particularly effective.

Zone-tillage methods may have more of an application further north. Here, a planting band 4 to 6 inches wide is tilled to around 4 inches deep into a killed cover crop, allowing the soil to warm up quicker in the spring. **Ridge-till** takes things a step further by hilling up bands of raised soil with discs or ridging wings, which then dry out and warm rapidly in the spring. Left in place for several seasons (avoiding the necessity for pre-plant tillage) soil from the top of the ridges is displaced by the planters and later restored by subsequent cultivations, helping to control weeds in the row.

Even so, reduced tillage methods generally rely on soluble chemical fertilizers to make up for the lessened biological activity caused by cold soil. The benefits are clear, however. Reduced tillage promotes soils with better tilth, higher moisture content (a problem in wet or clay soils), greater nutrient availability and bioactivity near the surface, and, finally, a much faster buildup of soil organic matter than conventional tillage and weed control methods.

One of the best outcomes of conservation tillage research for vegetable growers is the demonstrated value of hairy vetch. A hardy legume that generally overwinters well in the North, it is a copious nitrogen-fixer and nutrient enhancer that has particular affinity for tomatoes. Sown in early September (after first treating the seed with the specific bacterial inoculant), often with a nurse crop of oats to prevent frost heaving, it will become well established before winter's freeze and be off to a vigorous start in early spring. By tomato transplanting time in late May (Zone 5) it produces a dense biomass of tiny leaves and tendrils. Scalp-killed and kept as a mulch, or mowed and tilled into the soil, the vetch provides a well-balanced nutrient mix and a mellow, moisture-holding soil tilth for the crop.

Cultivators

The wide spectrum of cultivation equipment available today to fit specific crops can be highly confusing. Their efficacy depends on a wide variety of factors including soil type, terrain, cropping demands, price, and compatibility with your other equipment. They also require a systems approach utilizing highly accurate planters and straight rows to keep the crops out of harm's way of the cultivators later on. Adjustable rearview mirrors mounted just behind the tractor's front axle—giving the operator a continuous view of what is going on behind while they are driving forward— are a cheap but indispensable cultivation control tool.

In this regard, it's hard to beat the elegant simplicity of the old Allis Chalmers "G" cultivating tractor, manufactured in the late 1940s and early 1950s before being put out of business by the advent of the herbicide spray rigs. Many have been rebuilt and are still in regular use today. Lightweight and maneuverable with highly adjustable wheel spacings, the machines are easily adapted to bed or row culture. The engine sits behind the operator, giving an unobstructed view of the soil and the crop beneath. Hydraulically operated tool bars are easily mounted and interchanged to accommodate planters, fertilizer side-dressers, and a huge variety of cultivating tools. Modern counterparts manufactured today integrate the more available three-point hitch implements already on the market but the sublime unity of design and function of the "G" is somehow missing.

Hairy vetch

There are also a number of other, extremely able cultivating tractors made by various manufacturers still kicking around farm auctions and the backlots of implement dealers. The International Harvester Super A, for instance, has an offset engine up front, giving the operator a full view of the action of belly-mounted cultivators working the soil underneath. Unfortunately, old tractors have entered the rarified atmosphere of collectibles, where collectors will pay astronomical sums for old equipment, often driving up prices well beyond the reach of someone looking to actually farm with them.

Good resources

There's nothing like seeing particular units in action to gauge their effectiveness on your own farm. On-farm demonstrations and workshops are incredibly valuable. There are some excellent recent resources—a book and a video—to help with this task, providing detailed overviews of what is available and how they might (or might not) meet your particular needs.

Steel in the Field—A Farmer's Guide to Weed Management Tools, produced by the Sustainable Agriculture Network (SAN) and edited by Greg Bowman, is an extremely useful handbook. It not only describes a wide variety of cultivation equipment for all kinds of farming and crops, but also presents profiles of farmers and how they use the equipment for their specific cropping situations. Annotated line drawings clarify the details of each implement, and size and price comparisons put them in perspective. The easy-to-use book layout also cross-references the equipment to how it is used by the various farmers.

If a picture is worth a thousand words then a training video has got to equal several million. *Vegetable Farmers and Their Weed-Control Machines*, also produced by SAN in conjunction with Vermont Extension Specialist Vern Grubinger, goes to farms to interview farmers about their equipment and show it in action. For farmers, some of the camera angles alone are worth the purchase price, and it seems as if at least one camera must have gotten run over while making the film. Such up-close views focus on machine actions which may not be readily visible to operators or even observers in the field—you can almost see soil organic matter oxidizing before your eyes as the dirt flows like water in the wake of cultivator action. The video lets farmers (from all over the Northeast) speak for themselves about why they chose the equipment they use and what they hope to accomplish with it. A number of them recommend dedicating a tractor outfitted with specific cultivating arrays to permanent use for a specific task and using other tractors and equipment for other farming operations.

There is also a section on flame weeders, which is a valuable companion to descriptions in *Steel in the Field*. Stale seedbed, preemergent, and post-emergent weed flaming calls for highly honed management and safety skills and is not conducive to some situations. The system also calls for a lot of fine-tuning—too hot a flame, too close to the crops can be disastrous. It also calls for low residue/no residue tillage systems to reduce the fire hazard to begin with.

Five
Conclusions

ttitudes toward weeds and weediness run deep and many of them could do with some "weeding out." Negative perceptions of weeds are built into our language; are integral to our thinking; are even part of our aesthetic. Some mega-farmers are known for going through their fields one more time with herbicide to achieve the picture-perfect "clean" fields they have come to expect, even though the application has proven to be clearly inefficient—a waste of time and money in terms of substantive weed control. They are hardly alone; numbers of organic growers, too, subscribe to the mindset that the only good weed is a dead one.

To be sure, no matter how they are perceived, weeds must be properly managed to prevent them from outcompeting the crops—but management implies a working with, not necessarily annihilation or complete top-down control. The context is always that of whole ecological systems where a tweak or two over here will have impacts and ramifications over there and maybe elsewhere as well. Using the example of beneficial reduced-tillage practices, for instance, a farmer can immediately reduce weed emergence by not plowing the soil and maintaining a continuous cover between rows. However, over time any weeds that do make it to seed can rapidly build up a huge weed population at the soil's surface and lead to even greater weed pressure. High-residue cultivators therefore become an integral part of this particular system. In addition, killed cover crops or a compatible living mulch, such as grain rye or Dutch white clover, are well suited to physically suppress (via the mulch effect above ground) and chemically impact (via rye's allelopathic properties in the root zone) weed growth. They also significantly alter the soil's microenvironment to disrupt weed cycles to begin with. All of these are proven weed management practices. Put them all together in a systems approach and they take on synergistic proportions.

Wild yarrow

The key to weed management is to rethink your whole system, keeping the biological effects of all the concomitant practices first and foremost in mind—then try to minimize, as much as possible, the deleterious ones. Agriculture, of course, is not a natural process to begin with and everything we do has a relative impact, more or less severe. Yes, herbicides kill weeds, but their biocidal toxicity also stresses crop roots, impacts soil organisms, and contaminates water resources. Cultivation can work well but bare soil is highly erodible (there's no way around it), and it also creates a vacuum for more weeds to come in later. Most significantly, each pass with the cultivator oxidizes away organic matter and diminishes humus, like it or not.

One of the worst travesties of Industrial Agriculture is its near complete usurpation of the publicly funded research budget. Less than 0.1 percent of federally funded research projects have organic farming applications.[6]

While we are blessed with many high-caliber, biologically oriented researchers (many of them housed by IPM, Sustainable Ag, Extension, and Experimental Station programs), funding their work remains a constant problem. Furthermore, holistic systems are not easily analyzed under standard scientific protocol, and the necessary simultaneous co-investigation by scientists from different specialties and disciplines is almost nonexistent. Increasingly, too, researchers are under pressures to create products to patent and sell—a proprietary approach that very quickly can become self-serving. What is needed is more whole-system/practice-oriented research. What we often end up with are incomplete solutions done on a piecemeal basis with a limited value, after all.

It's interesting how Fukuoka's principles and some of the goals of conservation tillage intersect when it comes to weed management. It makes good biological sense to keep as much soil covered as much of the time as you can (permanently even, when using biostrips). "Weeds" also immediately cease to exist when they are no longer plants growing in the wrong place—they can become living mulch and habitat for beneficials. Just a few new contributions from the turf industry towards developing specific, non-competitive living mulch varieties, for instance, coupled with lighter, stronger, and less expensive high-residue and ridge tillers from manufacturers, could change how farmers farm and manage their weeds for the better—with far-ranging positive effects on erosion, soil quality, food safety, and the environment.

Until these diverse elements are readily available, small-scale system farmers can take advantage of winterkilled oats as a protective thatch which is strip- or ridge-tilled for planting come spring. Used in conjunction with biostrips between the beds or rows, the area left open to weeds, erosion, and tillage disruption shrinks considerably. Meanwhile, the system also creates a lush habitat for beneficials, providing definitive and ongoing pest control. Holistically, the soil is not only well protected, but organic matter content is greatly increased and humus renewed. A dynamic equilibrium establishes healthy soil and healthy plants. The previous symptoms of imbalance—weeds, pests, diseases, diminished soil fertility—fade in the process.

Finally, in order to determine where we're going, or even want to go, it's wise to consider where we've been and how that influences our consciousness. What follows is a take by Joseph Cocannouer, based on his work for many years with Southwest Native Americans and their agriculture:

> *Our colonial forefathers, with few exceptions, were industrialists. There were a few dirt farmers on the* Mayflower *and on subsequent ships, but as a rule the colonial settlers came from the small urban districts. They had been shopkeepers, small-business folk, preachers, teachers, lawyers.*
>
> *In the New World for a lengthy period there was little place for the shop as it had been known in Europe; not much place for even small business. Preachers and lawyers and teachers there were, who engaged in their professions, but even they had to turn to the soil for much of their living. And they looked upon their soil as little more than mechanical food factories. Machines of most kinds were primitive in those days, of course, but the machine mindedness was much like ours today. Cultivated land must be as clean as a shop counter. The Indians in a large measure were the agricultural teachers of our*

colonial parents. And the Red Man was a pretty keen agriculturalist. The colonialists declined to accept all of his 'crude' wisdom, however.

It is true that the Indian's Nature wisdom was mixed with superstition, but even so his agriculture was sound. It was sound because he listened to the subtle voices of the earth. Our forefathers acknowledged their God as the giver of gifts, but saw those gifts only as abundant harvests. The Indian gave thanks to his Great Spirit for the land that gave him his corn; the white man gave thanks for the corn. The one was a naturalist, the other an industrialist. And across the decades from that day until this our farmers have ever had their eyes on the corn, not on the soil that is responsible for that corn.[7]

Reference Notes

1. *Merriam-Websters Collegiate Dictionary*, 10th edition (Springfield, MA: Merriam-Webster, Incorporated, 1998).

2. Pfeiffer, E. E., *Weeds and What They Tell* (Emmaus, PA: Rodale Press, 1970), p. 10.

3. Cocannouer, J. A., *Weeds—Guardians of the Soil*, (New York: Devin-Adair, 1964), pp. 169–170.

4. Hampshire College Research Workshop, NOFA Summer Conference, 1997.

5. Stevens, W. K., "Sprawl Quickens Its Attack on Forests," *New York Times*, 7 December 1999, p. F6.

6. Lipson, M., *Searching for the 'O-Word'*, (Santa Cruz, CA: Organic Farming Research Foundation, 1997), p. 7.

7. Cocannouer, *Weeds—Guardians of the Soil*, pp. 171–72.

Bibliography

Abdul-Baki, A. A., and J. R. Teasdale. 1994. *Sustainable Production of Fresh Market Tomatoes with Organic Mulches.* Farmers Bulletin 2279, Washington, DC: USDA-ARS.

Bowman, G. (ed.) 1997. *Steel in the Field: A Farmer's Guide to Weed Management Tools.* Beltsville, MD: Sustainable Agricultural Network.

Cocannour, J. A. 1964. *Weeds—Guardians of the Soil.* New York: Devin-Adair.

Coleman, E. 1995. *The New Organic Grower.* White River Junction, VT: Chelsea Green.

Faulkner, E. H. 1943. *Plowman's Folly.* New York: Grosset and Dunlap.

Fukuoka, M. 1978. *The One-Straw Revolution.* Emmaus, PA: Rodale Press.

Fukuoka, M. 1987. *The Road Back to Nature—Regaining the Paradise Lost.* Tokyo: Japan Publishers.

Grubinger, V. and M. J. Else. 1994. *Vegetable Farmers and Their Weed-Control Machines* (video). Burlington, VT: University of Vermont Center for Sustainable Agriculture (available from SARE USDA, Northeast Region).

Northeast Organic Farming Association of New York, Inc. 1999. NOFA-NY *Organic Farm Standards and Administrative Procedures.* Binghamton, NY: NOFA-NY.

Pfeiffer, E. 1970. *Weeds and What They Tell.* Stroudsburg, PA: Bio-dynamic Farming & Gardening Assn., Inc.

Proceedings, 1999 New England Vegetable and Berry Conference and Trade Show. Portland, ME: University of Maine Cooperative Extension.

Sachs, P. D. 1993. *Edaphos—Dynamics of a Natural Soil System.* Newbury, VT: Edaphic Press.

Smith, M. (ed.) 1994. *The Real Dirt—Farmers Tell About Organic and Low-Input Practices in the Northeast.* Burlington, VT: Northeast Region Sustainable Agriculture Research and Education program.

Index

B

barley, 12
beans, fava, 17
beets, 26
bindweed, 3
Bio-Dynamic Association, 3
biostrips/strip insectary
    intercropping, 14–20, 49–50
bloodroot, 26
Bowman, Greg, 45
brassicas, 17–18, 33
broccoli, 31
buckwheat, 17
burdock, 7, 25
buttercup, 3

C

Canada thistle, 4, 25
carrot, wild, 4
carrots, 23, 26
chemical fertilizers, 12–13, 43
chickweed, 7
chicory, 3
chisel plows, 39
citrus, 12
clovers, 3
    as living mulch, 33–34, 36, 48
    natural farming techniques, use
        in, 12–13, 15, 17
Cocannouer, Joseph, 5–7, 50–51
coltsfoot, 3, 26

computer spreadsheets, 28
conventional agriculture. *See*
  industrial agriculture
cool-weather crops, 26–27
corn, 31–33
  herbicides, effect of, xi–xii
  herbicide-tolerant, xi
  natural farming techniques, use
    in, 13, 18
cornflowers, 3
cover crops, 5, 17, 25, 48
  herbicide-cleansing, xii
  as living mulches, 31–34, 48
  no-till, 16, 42
cowpeas, 17
crop residue, 19
crop rotation, 18, 27–28, 34
cultivation, to control weeds. *See*
  tillage, to control weeds
cultivators, 43–45, 48–49

D

daisy, 3
damp-off, 3
dandelion, 3, 7–9, 26
database, garden/farm, 27–28
diseases, control of, 3, 14
docks, 3
Dutch white clover, 33–34, 36, 48
dynamic plants, 3

E

earthworms, 14
eggplant, 35, 36
erosion, xi, 6, 16, 31, 32, 41–42, 48

F

fruit crops, 11–12, 35
Fukuoka, Masanobu, 11–13, 49

G

galinsoga, 21
garlic, 34
genetically engineered plants, xi
goldenrods, 3
greenhouses, diseases in, 3
gridders, 18
growing seasons, weeds as
  indicators of, 25–26
Grubinger, Vern, 45

H

hairy vetch, 17, 43, 44
henbit, vii–viii
herbicides, xi–xiii, 14, 42, 48
herbicide-tolerant crops, xi
herbs, x–xi, 7–8, 23
horsetail (*Equisetum arvense*), 3, 4
humus, 40–41, 49

I

industrial agriculture, xi–xiii, 1–2, 32, 37–39, 41
insects, beneficial, 8, 13, 14, 18
intersown crops, 11–13, 38–39. *See also* strip insectary intercropping/biostrips

K

kohlrabi, 17, 27

L

lambsquarters, 3, 7, 27, 33
leeks, 18
legumes, 33, 43
lettuce, 17, 19, 27
log, daily, 26, 27

M

map, farm/garden, 27–28
meadowsweet, 4
mechanization. *See* weedeating machines
medicinals, x–xi, 7–8
mosses, 4
mow and blow system, 19–20
mowing, to control weeds, 25

mulches, 19, 25, 28–36, 48
  living, 31–34, 48
  opaque solar film (plastic), 34–36
  soil, effects on underlying, 29–31
  supply of, 28–29
  weed seeds in, 29
mullein, 4
mustards, 4
mycorrhizae, 14, 19

N

natural farming techniques, 11–20, 49
  Japan, use in, 11–13
  mow and blow system, 19–20
  North America, use in, 13–14
  strip insectary intercropping/biostrips, 14–20, 49–50
nettle, 4, 7
nitrogen, 30, 32, 33, 43
no-till weed management, 16, 42

O

oats, 17, 34, 50
oats test, xii
One-Straw Revolution, The (Fukuoka), 11

onions, 26

organic certification programs, xiii

organic matter, 16, 32, 39–41, 49.
    See also cover crops; soil
        conditions

organic methods, research on, 49

P

perennial weeds, control of, 24–25

Permaculture concepts, 14

pest control
    natural farming techniques,
        12–14, 18
    plastic mulches, problems of, 36

pesticides, xii

pest production, secondary, xii, 14

Pfeiffer, Ehrenfried, 3–5

pigweeds, 3, 4, 27

plantains, 4, 33

planting times, weeds as indicators
    of, 25–26

plastic mulches, 35–36

poison ivy, 7

pollinators, 8, 18

potatoes, 18

pumpkins, 32, 33

purslane, 4, 7, 22

pussy willows, 26

Q

quackgrass, 4, 24–25

Queen Anne's lace, 19

R

ragweed, 4

raised beds, 15–20

rice crops, 11–13

ridge-till methods, 43, 50

Roundup Ready® soybeans, xi

rye, 12, 17, 31, 32–33, 48

ryegrass, annual, 17, 32, 36

S

soil conditions
    biostrips, use of, 15–17, 19
    machines, effect of, 39–41, 43
    mulches, effects of, 29–32
    specific weeds, preferred by, 3–4
    weeds, effects on soil of, 5–7,
        12–13

soil temperature
    mulches, effect of, 30–31, 35
    tillage methods, effect of, 42–43
    weeds as indicators of, 26

soil tests, 40

solar film, opaque, 35–36

soybeans, xi, 13

spinach, 17

spurge, 4

squash, 19, 32, 34

St. John's wort (*Hypericum spp.*), xi

stale seedbed weed control, 23

Steel in the Field—A Farmer's Guide to Weed Management Tools, 45

stirrup hoe, 23–24, 39

strawberries, wild, 4

strip insectary intercropping/ biostrips, 14–20, 49–50

strip-tillage, 39, 50

Sudax, xii

Sustainable Agriculture Network (SAN), 45

sweeps, 39, 42

T

thistles, 4, 24–25

Three Sisters agriculture, 38–39

tillage, to control weeds, 5, 25, 47–49

   conservation (reduced) tillage, 41–43

   negative effects of tillage, 39–40

   ridge-tillage, 43

   strip-tillage, 39, 50

   zone-tillage, 43

tomatoes, 19, 43

topsoil, xi

V

vegetable crops, 11, 13, 17–19, 34–35, 43

Vegetable Farmers and Their Weed-Control Machines, 45–46

W

water table, access to, 19

weed, to (defined), x

weed control strategies, 5, 21–36. *See also* weedeating machines

chemical, 5

   database, garden/farm, 27–28

   mulches (*See* mulches)

   perennial weeds, 24–25

   seedlings, control of, 22

   stale seedbed, 23

   stirrup hoe, 23–24

   timing crops to weed growth patterns, 26–27

weedeating machines, 37–46

   biological effects of machines, 39–40

   conservation (reduced) tillage, 41–43

   cultivators, 43–45, 48–49

humus, effect on, 40–41
information resources, 45–46
weeds
   defined, x–xi
   as enemy, 1–2
   as guardians of soil, 5–7
   as indicators, 3–5, 25–26
   as medicinals, x–xi, 7–8
   natural farming techniques,
      11–20, 49
Weeds: Guardians of the Soil
   (Cocannouer), 5
Weeds and What They Tell
   (Pfeiffer), 3–5

wheat, winter, 17
wild carrot, 4
wild strawberries, 4
winter grains, 11–13

yarrow, 4, 48

zone-tillage methods, 43

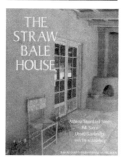